SAVAGE
PAGEANT

SAVAGE PAGEANT

BY

JESSICA Q. STARK

BIRDS, LLC
MINNEAPOLIS, NEW YORK, RALEIGH

Birds, LLC
Minneapolis, New York, Raleigh
www.birdsllc.com

Book design by Zoe Norvell

Cover art "The Tapir" by Anon
© The British Library Board (Add.Or.4973)
Cover design by Zoe Norvell

Library of Congress Control Number: 2019953699
Stark, Jessica Q
Savage Pageant / Jessica Q. Stark

First edition, 2020
ISBN-978-0-9914298-4-4
Printed in the United States of America

CONTENTS

ACT III | THE ANIMALS

Intermission

ACT IV | THE ILLNESS

Epilogue

Poems about saline and unsolicited advice

Poems about ghosts and the unhinged latch

Poems about sunsank and missing persons

Poems about dark matter on Google Maps

Poems about the crack and mass hysteria

Poems about restricted access and shelves for unmentionables

Poems about misinformation and contaminated waters

Poems about the wood before the stage

Poems about animals playing other animals without explanatory notes

Poems about stealing land and then putting your name on tombstones

Not-poems about song about poems

Songs about poems about song

Songs about poems about howls of unholding—an expanding context for love and flight

— Prologue —

Savage Pageant: A Genealogy

When   we were   little,

my sisters   (being the youngest, I too)   thought

     the pregnant   form   was disgusting.

Nothing is as   plain   or crass   as expecting:

     the awkward   roundness

     of past sex on   a body-stage
   and all that   skin x stretching x

What we really wanted   was

combustion   to burn the deed

around our own real estate.   What

we really wanted   was inelegant:

a clean break from   the spectacle

    with gas station snacks
    and water when we needed.

My grandmother had eleven pregnancies and
                          an infection.

My mother had four   and wished for boys.

Sometimes you can't put all the bones
back where they're supposed to go.

I had a boy and they took you out with a   knife.

THE SOIL

"The spectacle is an *affirmation* of appearances and
an identification of all human social life with appearances.
But a critique that grasps the spectacle's essential character
reveals it to be a visible negation of life—a negation that
has taken on a *visible form*."

—GUY DEBORD, *Society of the Spectacle*
(*La société du spectacle*), 1967

Jungleland:
A Genealogy, 1803-1915

1803:   Rancho El Conejo, a Spanish land grant in California, was gifted to José Polanco and Ignacio Rodriguez. Land grant titles were government-issued, permanent, and distributed to prominent men to encourage settlement in the area. The land was mostly devoted to cattle and sheep-raising. The owners of the ranchos frequently used Spanish-speaking Native American workers, many of them former mission residents, to till their newly acquired land. Native Americans report tyrannical tendencies in rancho owners and perform purification practices on the soil and the water used for farming, washing, and drinking. They warn of eventual drought in the territories. They bear within themselves a kind of aesthetics of hidden things. Rancho boundaries compose the basis of California's land survey system, and the names of ranchos remain on maps of the area today.

1874:   Egbert Starr Newbury purchases 2,259 acres and builds a home on the soil that would later be named Jungleland in the Conejo Valley of Southern California.

1877:   A severe drought bankrupts Newbury and the land is sold to the Crowley family. Part of the land retains his name. Newbury Park population: 37,775 (2010). Area code: 805. Highest elevation: 2,828 ft (862 m). Lowest elevation: 500 ft (200 m). Later address: 2522 Pleasant Way.

1910:   The Crowley family builds a five-bedroom, two-story house for the eldest son in the family, Frank, and his wife, Mae Casey Crowley. The house is later nicknamed the "Mother of Thousand Oaks," after serving as a hosting site for the first real estate office in the Conejo Valley's housing development. The Crowleys entertain prospective buyers that shuttle directly from downtown Los Angeles, serving dinner and providing a tour of the grounds, the oak trees, and its rabbits. Little is known about the Crowley family beyond their function in these first real estate ventures. To pave the way now for a phenomenology of what is hidden, one preliminary remark will suffice—an empty drawer is unimaginable. It can only be thought of. And for us, who must describe what we imagine before what we know, what we dream before what we verify, all wardrobes are full.

1911: Mabel Stark begins work with AI G. Barnes Circus in Culver City with animal trainers Al Sands and Louis Roth.

1915: President Woodrow Wilson commissions the first White House film screening of *The Birth of a Nation*. It is filmed on the property of what would later be named Jungleland. It would be frequently used as a recruitment tool for the Ku Klux Klan.

The House 12 Miles Away

for the maps to celebrity homes

We trek forests to

> dine with fine ghosts,

arrive before dawn

> to oak trees and

skittish rabbits and

two fewer specters than
> were advertised.

Are we disappointed?

We are disappointed.

The empty drawer

> holds more promise

than a known spool.
> Bare threads.

Before dining,

> we make sure

to touch their buttocks
> and the river stones

to determine

whether they might withstand another visit,

whether there is enough
water nearby with

which to rinse our tongue,

clear a throat—

THE DEAD LETTER OFFICE

We make an effort for some—

a shaky script, a single-digit slip of
ZIP code. But most times, they're

dead-on-arrival. Enclosed items
of value are carefully removed,

correspondence is destroyed to
protect customer privacy. Items

that cannot be returned are sold at
auction, except for firearms and porn.

Perhaps one day, you will know
what it's like to sit beside The Dead

Letter Office—a stunted hall of the
pending and untraceable plot.

Listen to this value, stranger, it is
the most important thing to know:

even the dead need to be touched
with hands—some human, some not.

Depending on where you stand,
you might become a window. But first:

to enter this domain, you need a
letter. For our trouble, a stamp.

And a shadow between rows will be
growing, like a blade of grass pressed

flat between pages of a book that was
miscounted in the vault's holding.

JUNGLELAND: SYMPTOMS

One Million B.C., Birth of a Nation,
Tarzan, The Ape Man, Jungle Jim,

A Tiger Walks, Bonzo Goes to College,
The Adventures of Robin Hood, Bomba,
The Yearling, Son of Kong, The Chimp,

Bedtime with Bonzo, Mr. Ed, The Call
of the Wild, Route 66, The Good Earth,
Dumbo, Circus Boy, I'm No Angel,

Dr. Doolittle.

The First White House Screening

Like writing history with lightning—
all sharp corners and dead-blind.
Jungleland bleaches its teeth for its
first high-house silver screening.
President Woodrow Wilson
smiles, recognizes the oak trees
mistaken for Southern reserve. A
litmus test for a better view, a cleaner
plot, a place to call one's own. Only.
Under President Wilson, a photo-
graph became required for all new
federal job applicants. The Navy, the
Treasury, but most importantly,
the Post Master General where,
shortly after election, ghosts
began floating behind screens.
An elegant solution: the details of
a look for a tidier exchange,
a salve for the face-to-face and the
averted eye. Your finest term
accomplishment: a population
of alternatives working hard under-
ground. The Dead Letter Office is
to the left, down the hall. Blank forms
tucked away from public view, an
envelope carrying the rust of bright
machinery away from the tongue. Not
dead, no trace. No one here by that
name. An easy opacity for the splice.
The imagination is most active
when the body is scared. I grasp

another letter, find your face
on the highest denomination of
our currency. *Sort to Destroy*, I
stamp it, but outside the reporters
are already getting it all wrong.

Area Four

You cannot clean up what you cannot see.

It has been ten years since I've lived on California soil—a decade, a block, an increment for generations. Geography accounts for memory as folds in a timeline; this map as undulation in something blackened, worn-out, and organized. I take the parchment and hike up to Rocketdyne—your favorite run—and it is hot, and I feel a dry gust at the ends of my fingers. The smell of shrubs that I used to feed pet rabbits. I choose a small spot at the top of a hill. There is sweat and soot on my upper lip that I can taste on my tongue. I bury the bond with my bare hands and fingernails because I have forgotten a tool. After I finish, I gaze at the plot from three different angles and decide it looks out-of-place and knowable. I place tough rocks and dead leaves over the top, but it's no use. I sit below an oak and breathe and try to picture trying again, but I all I can see is the hill that I sit on that is brown and yellow and gray and gray.

⁂

Their study compared the brain positron emission tomography (PET) scans of patients diagnosed with psychogenic dystonia, which caused painful muscle contractions in the leg, and patients with similar but organic, or explainable, dystonia of the leg, as well as those of healthy individuals. What they found was that both groups of dystonia patients had abnormal activity in the motor cortex of the brain, which controls voluntary movement, and the striatum, which acts as a relay station.

⁂

In 1959, thirty-five miles outside of Los Angeles at the Santa Susana Field Laboratory (Rocketdyne), one of the worst nuclear accidents in US American history occurred. Afterwards, workers at the site of the accident were ordered to open the release valve of radioactive contaminants into the air and the soil. Workers reported signing a document of confidentiality for their orders. Throughout the early 1960s, workers continued to release radiation into the sky through the exhaust stacks of at least three of Area Four's ten nuclear reactors. They disposed of barrels from reactors by taking them out to The Burn Pits, which released radioactive materials via smoke across the bodies of those ordered to dispose of the barrels. Many of the workers from The Burn Pits suffered asthma; nose bleeds; leukemia; pulmonary injuries; heart conditions; lesions; skin infections; chronic cough; and cancer of the lungs, skin, bone, and brain. "It's been eating me alive is what it's amount to," he said, "The others I've worked with are dead and gone."

TRACE LEAKAGE:
LA PET CEMETERY

Under the soil   is   another soil,

      holding bone   to   bone   to

trace substance,   leaking   rumors

      about   bad   timing   and

signatures.   It is

      waste   we breathe   that

we   drink but   cannot touch or

count   the number of   times

      we have   taken   in

this land   and   body,

thinking   a hole   (so simple)

might actually   forgive us   for

      what   was   left.

    We didn't   clean it up (have never)

but our hands   and tongues are

leaking,   and there is   so little time

    left   for   unburying it   alive.

— *Intermission* —

Name Numerology K-Hole: 11 Weeks

Hope is a thing with a name, and
   I am a personality calculator.

I hunted for you in Internet lists.
   This stranger sea—each route

too wayward by edge and vowel.
   A name is a settled home

for the indefinite. Unknown love-
   born, murky-watered babe, let

me call you Nothing. Mix in salt,
   melody, and ventilate. *Voilà*

elegy for an exact flaw, for self-
   knowing. We are only here for a

short time. You have ten fingers and
   ten toes, I have a black-and-white.

In it, your head is cast down from
   view, your face obscured.

ACT II

THE GHOSTS

"The admirable people in whom the system personifies
itself are well known for not being what they are;
they became great men by stooping below the reality of
the smallest individual life, and everyone knows it."

—GUY DEBORD, *Society of the Spectacle*
(*La société du spectacle*), 1967

JUNGLELAND: A GENEALOGY, 1919-1929

1919:   Louis Goebel arrives in Los Angeles and begins work at Gay's Lion Farm, butchering animal carcasses for food for the lions. But images do not adapt themselves very well to quiet ideas, or above all, definitive ideas. The imagination is ceaselessly imagining and enriching itself with new images.

1920:   Knott's Berry Farm opens in Southern California, which would contribute to rising competition between nearby amusement parks. What is a house without neighbors? A field without partition. The United States ratifies the nineteenth amendment, which grants women the right to vote.

1922:   Mabel Stark joins the Ringling Bros. and Barnum & Bailey Circus.

1920-26:   Gay's Lion Farm is relocated from Los Angeles to El Monte. Louis Goebel does not follow his employer. He begins working at Universal Studios in the studio zoo as a meat cutter, feeder, and groundskeeper for its celebrity animals. Carl Laemmele, owner of the studio at the time, eventually disposes of the studio's zoo after poor profits. Louis Goebel purchases six lions from the defunct zoo. For the present, we shall consider the images that attract.

1925:   Having failed to find affordable land in the Los Angeles County region, Louis and Kathleen Goebel purchase 170 acres in Thousand Oaks from the Crowley family property, or five lots for $10 each. Total plot: $50.

1926:   Louis and Kathleen Goebel build Goebel's Lion Farm on their newly acquired land.

1927:   For publicity, MGM studio tours a lion named Jackie—billed as Leo the Lion—in a modified Ryan Brougham plane with tanks for milk, water, and extra fuel, with a cage incorporated in the body of the small aircraft to house Jackie as she flew. A sign accompanied her flight: MGM Leo, the Flying Lion.

1928:   Five hours into the plane ride from San Diego to New York, Jackie's plane crashes in the Arizona desert. The pilot, Martin Jenson, leaves the lion in the cage to seek help. Jackie is left with a small supply of milk, sandwiches, and water. The surrounding trees are quite straight and give the impression of standing guard over the lion's house. Martin was found four days later. Rescuers recover Jackie after a week's search. She is unharmed and earns the nickname, "Leo the Lucky." I should say: the house shelters day-dreaming; the house protects the dreamer; the house allows one to dream in peace.

1928:   Mabel Stark begins working with tigers in the John Robinson Show. In this year, she would suffer her worst mauling. She suffered a wound that almost severed her leg, face lacerations, a hole in her shoulder, and a torn deltoid. She said she lost her footing.

1929:   Responding to interest of passing visitors wanting to see the lions, Louis and Kathleen Goebel begin admitting the public in exchange for a fee. Admittance: $.50. Here, then, is a rapid account of the chapters that compose this book.

TRACE LEAKAGE: JUNGLELAND

Anonymous on 2016-06-14 said:
I just watched an old Route 66 and it was about this lion park circa 1966. The show was, hell is empty, all the devils are here.... Filmed at this location! Enjoy.

Anonymous on 2016-06-29 said:
Wow! Reading all these comments is like a walk down memory lane. I didn't live in TO, but my aunt and uncle did. My uncle owned a garage called Newberry Park Automotive. I remember going out there as a kid and passing by Jungleland and begging my mom to take me there, every time we drove past. GOD she must've been sick of hearing it. Reading all the comments with stories about the old place, brought back a lot of great memories. Thanks!

Anonymous on 2013-06-28 said:
Spotted a jet-black cougar in Lake Hughes, California 4/2012. It could have been something else. I am just calling it a cougar because the area is known to have them.

Anonymous on 2014-11-24 said:
I have several pictures of my dad with the lions at Goebels. He used to work with them. He is laying on the grass in front of the lion cages. He is with a lion and you can see others still in their pen. He worked with Johnny and liked him a lot. He used to climb the trees and test the ropes that Johnny swung from.

Anonymous on 2014-07-12 said:
Does anyone remember a baby elephant named Ruth owned by Slivers Madison at Jungleland about 1961 to 1963? If so, do you have photos? She would have been maybe three to five years old.

Anonymous on 2014-06-09 said:
Wow, I need to take some time to read all the comments since I last posted in 2008 about Zoltan's mauling. Good memories!

Anonymous of CALIF on 2013-03-10 said:
I WAS ABOUT 5-6 YEARS OLD WHEN MY GRANDPARENTS
HARRY & KATIE HARTUNG HAD THE RESTERAUNT AT THE
FRONT OF THE LION FARM. I RECALL THERE WERE LIVE
ANIMAL SHOWS THERE ON THE WEEKENDS. I BELEIVE
A MAN NAMED LOUIS ROTH WAS THE ANIMAL TRAINOR
AND HIS DAUGHTER PERFORMED WITH THE TIGERS. I RE-
CALL GRANDMA WAS SHOCKED TO SEE MAE WEST BEING
SO SHORT WHEN PORTRAYED IN THE FILMS AS QUITE TALL.
I LOVED FEEDING THE BABY LIONS. I HAVE SOME PICTURES,
ONE OF CLARK GABLE WHO WAS VISITING, VERY FOND
MEMORIES OF BYGONE DAYS.

Anonymous on 2007-03-27 said:
another bit of info. Jane Manfield famous back in the 60's well her son was
mauled by a lion at Jungleland.

Anonymous on 2009-10-28 said:
I lived in Thousand Oaks from 1961 to 1966 and remember going to Jungle
Land many times. One morning in the fog my dad almost ran his 57 Buick
in to a bunch of Elephants on the Ventura highway on their way to a movie
set. No freeway yet and we could walk there from our house. Have not been
back to Thousand Oaks in over 40 years.

Anonymous on 2010-12-03 said:
Hi Great site of history! Does anyone remember an elephant that had the tip
of one of his tusks broken off?

Anonymous on 2007-03-27 said:
Its me again. Its a shame you dont have pictures of Jungleland or TO back in
the day. as for the panther. I remember when it got loose and we the kids had
to stay inside I think for a day or two, but I also remember that they shot the
panther and killed it. I'm thinking if you really wanted to know it still has to
be in the newspaper at the Liberty.

Anonymous on 2010-05-22 said:

I remember going to Jungleland! It was awesome. I would love to see a book written and a memorial built. I also remember when the John Strong Circus came to Orcutt. They performed in the Orcutt Jr High Gym. it was the first circus I had ever seen and I was enthralled.

Anonymous on 2012-08-01 said:

I was there and saw the lion attack him.the lion was on a chain staked down the kid walked to close to the lion and the lion jump him and had his head in his mouth.witch totally freak me out.the trainer grab the lion in a head lock and pulled the lion jaws apart to release him out of the lions mouth. as a kid in those days what better place to hang out at. And i lived two blocks from jungle land.that day they were filming were the action is a dick clark dance show.sonny and shair and paul revier and the raders were there too.... wow what a day

Anonymous on 2014-08-17 said:

wow what memories i grew up in newbury park , and recently found a wooden chicken with a saddle on it from jungle world its awsome looking very old, might be worth someting?

WORLD JUNGLE COMPOUND
for the weeds

Ten-minute songs, or
the ineluctable line

between the sublime
and torture.

You, Louis Goebel:
expert meat-

striker for hungry cats.
Carried drip-organs on

hand for Hollywood jaws.

Jungleland, he whis-
pered, whiskered-one

evening, attending to
his favorite paws.

At his height, he wore
the pelts of his masters.

Women got hot, think-
ing, how many more?

Blood under nail-
sod, fleece cast out

with the refuse. After
a spell, they wearied

of dark-stilled
bottled sweets.

He died alone beside a
Macintosh, an old shoe.

Cops and Robbers

The Boone Society, the Devon Record Office, and other hired British genealogists have not been able to find a birth, marriage, or death record for this George Boone of England.

Or another game, but   same   lines
    in the sand   like

tie me up and leave   me cold,   like

    I'm the bad one,   bad one, I know. Hands
falling again on   silent   alarm

while the hills outside   rustle,   restless
    rabbits greet   familiar scripts:

    five students   in my classroom with
the same sickness   like

    five students   in my   classroom
with   the same   white lie: California's

        elementary lessons,   or how to   tie one's lineage

        to Daniel Boone,   how to erase   one's
face completely   in the dirt   and heel of history's

        dead   darlings.   Never heard of him,   I say,

shifting wrists under   tacky rope   tied tight to
    an oak   tree   the sun   sinking

behind   the hill   the trees,   like stoic captors,

        holding their roots   firmly   in place

A Note for Mabel, Mabel, Tiger Trainer

The root of entertainment
is the ruse of control.

Tigers are wild animals; un-
hook the latch on the eyelet.

*"Most of all I was concerned for the audience.
I knew it would be a horrible sight if my body
was torn apart before their eyes."*

—MABEL STARK, *Hold That Tiger*

Mabel Stark worked for the Al G. Barnes circus, Ringling Bros. and Barnum and Bailey Circus, Sells-Floto Circus, Paramount, and Jungleland. In 60 years of working with large cats, she was mauled and hospitalized 17 times. She wrote an autobiography and had a pet tiger. She married five times and overdosed on barbiturates in Thousand Oaks, California, after getting fired from her final tiger taming job for her age. In September, I met my first Mabel and wondered if you were buried in her vocal cords. She introduced herself as a pharmacist. When I shook her hand, I shook your ghost in reverie. Watching you walk away felt like touching wet bricks. Perhaps there are no accidents. Maybe there are a multitude of strings attached at the tips of our fingertips from now to a deeper cut from a past or future frame. Every taste electric, every light another piece. Every shadow a notion of what was, every title—yours. I stand in a bookshop aisle, look to my right, and find it.

REAL LIVE RUMORS

Not a fact. Not a lock
left unlatched. Not the
kind of city where you
should. Not a detail.
Not an unopened note.
Not a punctuation. Not an
error. Not a last resort.
Not a misspelling nor a
slip of the tongue.

This is a moth caught in
a strange flash and bulb.
This is a blank slate of dream,
filled with unmentionables.
This is a cat with odd toes
and a nice look. A home in
a suburb filled with longshots—
an unhurried portrait, a whisper
of a friend, secrets written
on the table after dark.

DANIEL BOONE'S BONES

Forensic science, what a bother.

A little know-how and you've
lost the fairytale. Exhumed

dirty limbs only to reveal
the not-so features of another.

Pieces of your architecture
we pull from the ground:

a tall man (not you),
a black man (not you),

another unmarked grave.

Certainly not the boon
we sought—a reenactment

statue, a gated stone, a hole
to place a flower with a note.

Dear Daniel Boone, I love
you more than I love this

carnal species. For your
silence, a plastic crate.

For your clavicle, a duplicate
entrance. Your appendages

lying exactly nowhere on a map—
the greatest commemoration for

this tall, flat site of reversals.

And no territories to separate
and no corpse to fear or prize.

Your body: a procession of ants
scattering across bright white.

MISS PHOTOFLASH

for Jayne Mansfield

Where do you sleep tonight,
Vera Jayne Palmer?

A heart-shaped pool,
a wayward corridor, a pink
penchant for gone-wrong.

Working-class Monroe,
Blonde Ambition,

Great Tail Switch,
Broadway's Smartest Dumb.

Attach a name to fix you
and keep you known.

To my silver screen ladies:

yell five straight hours to get
a husky voice, the sexy kind.

Fill a stage with anatomy, but
don't forget your expiration

& cultivate a showy end.

Source a rumor-gone-wrong, a
small flirtation with a fiend—

each highway leading
towards closing credits,

premature.

But the children were
safe, and the photograph—

Promises! Promises!

Your final joke:

a white wig on the road,
left out loud.

"You know which title I like best?"

"I like to be called mother."

Zoltan Hargitay
Was a Telephone

Zoltan walked into the lion's cage and was bitten on the neck by the lion. Zoltan ran from his mother, Jayne Mansfield, into the lion's cage and was bitten on the neck by the lion. Zoltan, able to fit between the cage's bars with his small stature, squeezed into the lion's cage unnoticed and was bitten on the neck by the lion. Zoltan, having been left unattended for several hours by his mother, Jayne Mansfield, was standing outside of the lion's cage when he was bitten on the neck by the lion. Zoltan was accompanied by an experienced lion trainer and his mother, Jayne Mansfield, in the lion's cage when he was suddenly bitten on the neck by the lion. Officers report that a scheduled feeding had been missed, which may have prompted the lion to bite Zoltan, son of Jayne Mansfield, on the neck. Bystanders say they witnessed Zoltan biting the tail of another lion just moments before he was bitten on the neck by the offending lion. Zoltan had forgotten a toy in the lion's cage and ran back to retrieve it and was bitten on the neck by the lion. Jayne Mansfield, mobbed by a number of photographers during her latest visit to Jungleland, reportedly lost track of her son when he walked into the lion's cage and was bitten on the neck by the lion. Sources were unable to retrieve comment from Jayne Mansfield on the details leading up to her son's neck injuries. Shortly after the attack, the lion was immediately shot and removed from the park.

— Intermission —

A. Know Your Symptom: 17 Weeks

mild cramping and spotting, missed period,
fatigue, nausea, tingling or aching breasts,
frequent urination, bloating, motion sickness,
mood swings, temperature changes, extreme
fatigue and heartburn, food aversions, acne,

contempt from strangers, faster heartbeat,
decreased libido, high blood pressure, breast
and nipple changes, noticeable weight gain,
low back ache, breast tenderness, leg swelling,
flatulence, heightened allergies, leakage of urine,
shortness of breath, leg cramps, headaches,
sensitivity of olfactory senses, increased libido,
constipation, diarrhea, vaginal discharge,
mild uterine cramping, stuffy nose,

contempt from loved ones, lightheadedness,
hot flashes, thirst, moodiness, dizziness,
frequent urination, lowered immune system,
metallic taste, insomnia, rash, sleeplessness,
brain fog, depression, hemorrhoids, bleeding
gums and noses, vivid dreams and nightmares

B. Know Your Symptom: 17 Weeks

Symptomatology, inclusive of
but not limited to, women
being vicious to other
women—small lion circling a
cage. Your missed feeding is

a sorry excuse for the tooth-
gnash and the bitter scent.

Deliver water to cat, adverse
and opaque. Your tedium on
display for a finer feast and claw.

What the eye knows, but
 refuses most when reading
the headlines of strangers:

lies float up to the surface, a
sunset strikes again on cue.

Taming tigers takes striking
out borders in the body—
tender ribcage cutting breath.

This fine body of sediment,
a reduction of the narrative
and the easy tabloid. What
better way to feel estranged
from blood than separate
its liquid into tiny rows?

Frozen cubes, air-taut.

Know your symptom, she said,
and plucked another limb
from the crowd, her ears
perched for ready applause.

ACT III

THE ANIMALS

"The spectacle is not a collection of images, but
a social relation among people, mediated by images."

—GUY DEBORD, *Society of the Spectacle*
(*La société du spectacle*), 1967

JUNGLELAND: A GENEALOGY, 1930-1951

1930-33: Louis Goebel begins purchasing other exotic animals for his compound. He attaches elephants and occasionally other animals to the side of the road leading from and to Los Angeles as advertisement of his quickly developing zoo. The elephants' large stature was particularly effective at catching the attention of those traveling by the grounds. Everything, even size, is a human value.

1932: To make sure his lions were used for *Tarzan, the Ape Man* (1932), Louis Goebel camps out at the film site near Lake Sherwood in Ventura County. Thus, the spiraled being, who, from outside, appears to be a well-invested center, will never reach his center. His lions feature in this film and would be featured in many others to follow.

1934: Louis Goebel requests to use the phrase, "Home of the MGM Leo the Lion," on ashtrays to sell at his zoo. Leo's real name now is Slats, but he will assume other names, as new lions replace the need for the image of Leo the MGM Lion to continue in Hollywood up until the 1950s.

1935: Louis Goebel changes the name of Goebel's Lion Farm to Goebel's Wild Animal Farm to more accurately depict its expanding inventory. Elephant rides: $.75. At this time, the grounds housed 43 lions, 4 leopards, 6 camels, and 1 tiger. But what a spiral man's being represents! And what a number of invertible dynamisms there are in this spiral! One no longer knows right away whether one is running toward the center or escaping.

1938: Mabel Stark begins working at Goebel's Wild Animal Farm, where she becomes the first US American, female tiger tamer to front her own show.

1940:   On July 8th a barn catches fire and, fueled by the Santa Ana winds, spreads through Goebel's Wild Animal Farm. Beauty and magnitude cause spores to swell. In a panic from the burns, an elephant runs and breaks the property's main water line, making it difficult to contain and extinguish the fire. The cause of fire was reported as a result of spontaneous combustion.

1941-45:   Louis Goebel, trying to recover from financial strain caused by fire destruction to his inventory, buys and sells exotic animals from the site of Goebel's Wild Animal Farm. During this period, he supplies most of the rhesus monkeys used in the development of the polio vaccine. He acquires and sells an apex of 26 elephants in the span of a few months. When we accept slight amazement and, in the world of the imagination, it becomes normal for an elephant, which is an enormous animal, to come out of a snail shell. It would be exceptional, however, if we were to ask him to go back into it.

1945:   Two-year-old Donnie Fletcher is mauled and killed by the Goebels' pet panther on Pleasant Way Drive. The United States deploy two nuclear bombs on Hiroshima and Nagasaki, Japan.

1946:   Due to financial duress, Louis Goebel sells his compound to animal importer, Trader Horne, and Billy Richards, the manager of AI G. Barnes Trained Wild Animal Circus. We are the diagram of the functions of inhabiting that particular house, and all the other houses are but variations on a fundamental theme. The word habit is too worn a word to express this passionate liaison of our bodies, which do not forget, with an unforgettable house. The two re-name the property World Jungle Compound.

1947:   The North American Aviation corporation, which amassed power in WWII by producing more aircrafts than any other weapons company, opens a 2,800-acre nuclear test site in Ventura County in California's Conejo Valley.

1951:   Peggy, a chimpanzee from the World Jungle Compound, stars in *Bedtime for Bonzo* alongside Ronald Reagan. One of the most obedient and well-trained of the World Jungle Compound's chimpanzees, Peggy unexpectedly attempts to choke her co-star by his necktie and must be tranquilized on set. The necktie, pulled so tightly, has to be cut off of Ronald Reagan's neck with a pair of scissors.

STRANGE BEASTS
for miscalculation

With all the morning
bees we caught
fleeing from
ziplocks held high
above our heads I felt
lighter than a
pixie dust chugging
contest in the back
of third period
waiting for Mr. Fletcher
to turn us out for a
better office Didn't you-
know the way I shook
the time the leaves
talked back to me
outside Pierce Hall
the way the petals of
each dandelion juror
unfurled to reveal
these strange beasts
we taught the things
we called bees to float
up into the sky to burst
into individual
bundles of paper
to carry our notes
downward down
back towards the
dirt of the Earth
back towards the
ground below
our boots to sprout
something bigger

than both of us
some creature
too large for
those plastic bags
to contain

Leo at MGM

is buried on former Jungleland
soil, now known by another name.

Neon glowworm sitting

pretty on ticky-tack-taste.

Garland-cocky in the wake
of another storm. One talon,

one record of criminality,
one dimming star.

Another name.

The sunshine yields to
hard rain, day five.

Here is a piece to peel
and then toss:

this ornate carpet falls on sharp
cracks—try to forget who you are.

A displaced name is a
casualty.

And no more poems
for you.

And no more flash.

Just a few sandwiches left
in the slats of your cage.

For seven days in the
Arizona sun, you wait—

ROADSIDE ATTRACTIONS

FADE IN:
INT. THEATER – DAY, SEVEN DAYS LATER
(Corky, Bimbo, and Newscaster)

CORKY ENTERS STAGE WITH BIMBO THE ELEPHANT.
CORKY WEARS A SHINY YELLOW AND RED SUIT THAT
MATCHES BIMBO'S TASSELS AND HEADDRESS. THEY BOW
TO TENTATIVE APPLAUSE.

CORKY

Hollywood loves its orphans—
elephant replacing elephant,

no time for a new name.

The first assumes apparition.

We rub a smudge out of glass,

hope for a less rowdy beast
with a more (whispers) typical size.

Chain toe to highway, before 101—
a sight to see to catch a few flies.

The African elephant's nails are
worn down. A thick layer above

that refuses shock, absorbs others.

Species of mothers, this is a
sorry stage for your kind.

Take the Baby Ruth, Bimbo,

wish yourself a shorter

lifespan, and save yourself
the bitter care of rootrub.

We are a sullen lot, we agree.

We take image after image
for a sharper set of teeth:

the voice like a cheese grater,
the cat-and-mouse outlaw.

A hint of a human smile, we hope
for most when touching a

new stage, this slick-oil-
lovelorn trap for new tricks.

And still, we've memorized the
fib—we rearrange the ghosts.

Like the way Daniel Boone's son's
grave says, "Killed by Indians,"

and we laugh without saying it
and wish we could ever really

abandon the premises—leave
the evidence under a new name.

FADE OUT:

<u>EXT. COSTUME STORE, DAY</u>

In the heart of West Los Angeles, a shop's large OPEN sign glows.

N 34° 10.362 W 118° 50.772

There were six original lions at Goebel's Lion Farm: Andy, Min, Bill, Momma, Poppa, and Little Caesar.

Newbury Park High School

Conejo Valley conduit, AKA

Dear teleology of activity:

"A panther has escaped" &
stalks the Shell nightly

Toe-to-palm
Wind/struck

Cat-and-Mouse outlaw,
settling for acne with a badge.

"I was really scared,"
Curtis told deputies.

It just sat there, staring
at me with yellow eyes.

Striking, foul—
a diversion

leasing nightly tirades:
"Disneyland w/ live animals."

Unhappy, they acknowledge,
but still they adore the roster:

Yolanda Washington
Judy Miller
Lissa Kastin

Dolly
Cepeda

& Real
Live Lions.

More daily victims
lack tongue
lack mal/feasance

"We are and then we aren't,"

Curtis told deputies,
"I was really scared."

White hair,
clean lines,

White heat,
his Domain.

Curtis comes in,
the cars roll out

But the panther—

"Ten Years," they cry,

roams freely and
*some*thing ought

to be done about
such loosely held

strands in these
damp, dark days.

Black Panther Plays Game of 'Cat and Mouse'

By NICK NIELSEN

*~~ phantom black panther ~~~~~~~~~~
~~~~~ of Ventura County ~~~~~~~~~ re-
appeared ~~~~~~~~~~~~~~~~~~~~~~~~~~
~~~~~ a teen-age security guard ~~~~~~~
~~

~~~~~~~~~~~~~~~~~~~~~~~~~~~~~
~~~ "mouse" ~~~~~~~~~~~~~~~~~~~~
~~~~~~~~~~~~~~~~~~~~~~ there staring at
~~~~~~~~~~ green-yellow eyes.
~~~~~~~~~~~~~~~~~~~~~~~~~~~
~~~~~~~~~~~~ exclusive housing development
~~~~~~~~~~~~~~~~~~~~~~~~~~~~
~~~~~~~~~~~~~~~~~~~~~~~~~~~~~
25 yards away.*

THE END OF THE AUCTION

met with little praise—no
fireworks or final meals.

Boxes of fur snap down
rough roads. Paper posters

lining stone. A small price

for a lot of lions, a bargain
for a lot of beast. Seek this

cat, known from an early
cast. Or this one, dumb

but plain-pretty around
the tooth and nail. The

final hour brought out
the most desperate acts.

Oak table with purchase of
an ordinary chimpanzee.

A lock of hair, your hand.

At dusk, an ice cream truck
played Rudolph in October.

We are on short duration
with these distractions.

Everything is electric in
finitude. Your smile, this

habit, these trees—greenest
when set against the grain

of a new season. But the
sleep was so good, and the

dream—a better medicine
than all the songs we had

memorized for the stage.

— *Intermission* —

Savage Pageant: 33 Weeks

for the panther, escaped

[**ley**-ber] noun

1.productive activity, especially for the sake of economic gain.
2.the body of persons engaged in such activity, especially those work-
ing for wages.
3.this body of persons considered as a class (distinguished from manage-
ment and capital).

Last week I felt your hiccups
for three days straight. This week,

unknown. A collection of impulses—
this savage page. I pay to sit

with a circle of strangers to feel
more prepared and one woman

cries. I feel my eyes roll and
I curl into another language.

I am obsessed with hiding my own
nakedness. The body on display:

a public domain of choices made—
a needle, a drink of sugar, the sun

going down when I rise. Is it madness
to have you? Elephants breaking

the main water line. There are
things I'd like to tell you before

you are born: like don't ever sit
in circles with strangers, like

you don't always have to be in
motion to survive, like the human

heart is capable of making the
head feel very small. And the

last tissue I'll give you, before
giving you away to the clock

and the stars, is a simple one:
already you are part of the air

and this end will not summarize
forever. Stay static, for a time,

and hold onto the slippery pull
of hearsay, rumor—these legends.

Even if they are stones, they are
made of sand. And even if you can't

jump ship, you might not
need to find your way home.

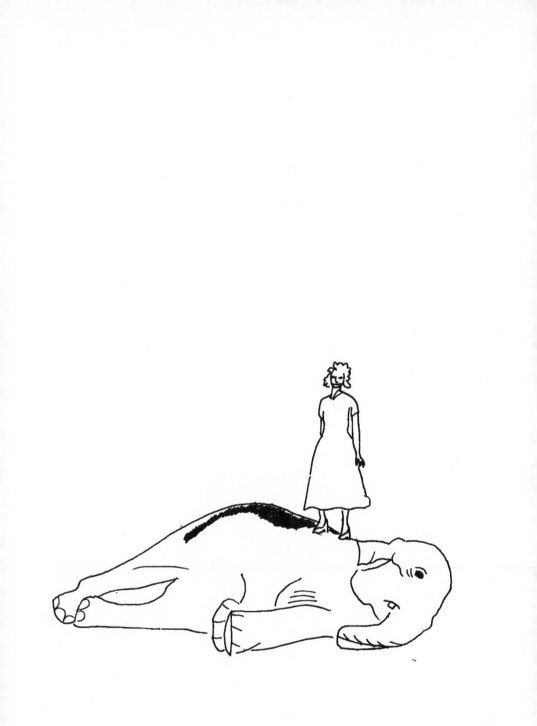

ACT IV

THE ILLNESS

"When the real world is transformed into mere images,
mere images become real beings—figments that provide
the direct motivations for a hypnotic behavior." "But a lie
that can no longer be challenged becomes insane."

—GUY DEBORD, *Society of the Spectacle*
(*La société du spectacle*), 1967

JUNGLELAND:
A GENEALOGY, 1956-1969

1956:   The property is sold to Sid Rogell and James Ruman, employees
         of 20ᵗʰ Century Fox. They rename the compound Jungleland
         and announce plans to include reproductions of African, Asian,
         and Middle Eastern jungles, with the introduction of a mar-
         ketplace and bazaar offering over 100 concessions. At times
         when we believe we are studying something, we are only being
         receptive to a kind a of day-dreaming. They attain data from
         the Stanford Research Institute and dream of a tramway. They
         describe their plan as "a kind of Disneyland with Live Animals."

1959:   Employees release an unknown amount of radioactive gases
         into the atmosphere during a partial nuclear meltdown at the
         Sodium Reactor Experiment in Ventura County, California to
         avoid a full nuclear meltdown. Unrecorded amounts of radiation
         are expelled from the reactor for weeks after the accident and
         the evidence of such is continually destroyed in The Burn Pits.

1960:   Highway 101 opens the Ventura Freeway, directing the majority
         of traffic away from the site of Jungleland.

1961:   Louis Goebel reacquires Jungleland through foreclosure after
         struggling business under Sid Rogell and James Ruman. All
         ownership of the property and animals revert back to Goebel
         with the transfer of a single document. It is our task, too, to
         sensitize the document by multiplying its variations.

1962:   Three episodes of "mass hysteria," or psychogenic illness, occur
         worldwide during this year: the Tanganyika laugher epidemic,
         the June bug epidemic, and a fit of psychogenic seizures in Welsh,
         Louisiana. In the Tanganyika laughter epidemic, 60 schoolgirls,
         aged 12-18, could not stop laughing for up to six months. They
         said things were moving in their minds, ungovernable things.

1963:   One of the four panthers housed at Jungleland escapes his cage. A two-year-old black panther, considered extremely dangerous, remains at large in the Thousand Oaks area and would never be recovered to his owners. Rilke once wrote: 'These trees are magnificent, but even more magnificent is the sublime and moving space between them, as though with their growth it too increased.' Over a ten-year period after his escape, local newspapers periodically report occasional sightings of the panther outside of truck stops or gas stations neighboring the hills. The co-owner of Jungleland offers a reward for the cat, $1,000, dead or alive.

1964:   Roy Kabat and Thurston "Tex" Scarborough assume responsibility of Jungleland as joint park managers. Within this year, they take 100 percent ownership. Kabat buys Chucko the Clown for birthday parties. They spend $90,000 on the Sky Glide tram. If we attain to the limit at which dream becomes exaggerated, we experience a sort of consciousness of constructing the house, in the very pains we take to keep it alive, to give it all its essential clarity. The petting zoo is expanded.

1966:   Tex Scarborough is attacked by a lion, resulting in partial amputation. Here, as elsewhere, life is energetic at its summit.

1966:   Zoltan Hargitay, Jayne Mansfield's son, is mauled by a tiger at Jungleland and remains in critical condition for several weeks. In an effort to save her son's life, Jayne Mansfield's meets with the occultist Anton LaVey days after the accident for help. Intimate photographs of LaVey and Mansfield surface in her Pink Palace shortly after their meeting and incite public scandal. In the intimate harmony of walls and furniture, it may be said that we become conscious of a house that is built by women from the inside, since men only know how to build a house from the outside, and they know little or nothing of the "wax" civilization. Zoltan miraculously recovers from his life-threatening injuries. Jayne Mansfield attains a $1.6 million-dollar settlement for the attack. The lawsuit significantly contributes to Jungleland's bankruptcy.

1967:   Slowly the tray took on a dull luster. Jayne Mansfield, along with her lover Sam Brody, die in a car accident en route to New Orleans. The accident was caused in part by a dense fog from an anti-mosquito spray that obstructed views. According to the police report, "the upper portion of the white female's head was severed." Although it was rumored that she was beheaded during the accident, scalping is a closer description to her fate. Her three children in the vehicle are unharmed.

1968:   Mabel Stark is fired from Jungleland. The same year, she commits suicide three months after hearing of her favorite tiger's escape, capture, and death.

1969:   How wonderful it is to really become once more the inventor of a mechanical action! And so when a poet rubs a piece of furniture—even vicariously—when she puts a little fragrant wax on her table with the woolen cloth that lends warmth to everything it touches, she creates a new object; she increases the object's human dignity; she registers this object officially as a member of the human household. Roy Kabat and Tex Scarborough enter voluntary bankruptcy. On October 8, Jungleland holds an auction on-site for the sale of its animals. More than 1800 animals were sold. Hippopotamus: $450. Single tiger: $750. Rare tortoise: $7500. An orangutan and its mate: $10,000. Jungleland closes its doors shortly after auction.

❧

After having followed the day-dreams of inhabiting these uninhabitable places, I returned to images that, in order for us to live in them, require us to become very small, as in nests and shells.

ARIEL

With hair up-staring—then, like, like
reeds, not hair—
Was the first man that leaped, cried, "
Hell is emptyAnd all the devils are here."

—Shakespeare's *The Tempest*

Darkness grew a little finger
       and led the company

of men into the sea. Driven mad with
       the after-places of memory:

the trace substance,   the years
       of sleep roused by the crack.

There was nowhere else to go
       but over   they cried.

There were no   instructions on
       how   to create an illusion.

So swiftly inside a storm they recall:

a spirit released from   prison
       for service was still   a

prisoner.   The ship   and its rich

       garments were breaking apart.

Mass Psychogenic Illness: ~~A phenomenon in which~~ social trauma ~~or anxiety~~ combined with a suspicious event ~~to produce psychosomatic symptoms,~~ such as ~~nausea, difficulty breathing, and paralysis. Emerging theories source~~ environmental toxicity and proximity to hazardous waste ~~dump sites as a related cause of symptoms. If many~~ individuals ~~come to~~ believe ~~that~~ the psychosomatic outbreak is ~~connected to the cause of the~~ trauma ~~or anxiety, these symptoms can~~ spread rapidly throughout a population.

THERE ARE MANY TYPES OF CANNIBALS

Hatch a plan; break a
       windshield.

Find the culprit:

a change in climate,
       bad water,

more bad water, traffic.

An imaginary sniper

       breaking glass

while dogs sleep.

Low-flying military

       crafts making better

news than the misread

       routine and

the usual percentage

       of broken glass.

A ghost is a felt

       miscalculation

in the overflow of human

information and category—

       reserve a space

for the crack. Look

       through

perfect symmetry for

some bright triangle

       in misty air.

If you don't think

       of the car

or the dogs, or the

water, you might

miss not knowing.

There is no one out

       in the street.

Now look again.

MASS PSYCHOGENIC ILLNESS

for the archive

And another thing: the 60s
        were a great year for mass hysteria.

        Tanganyika schoolgirl ('62),
and a joke gains wind, loses origins.

Traveled downhall, he said,
        pursed the chalkboard.

By the thousand, I
            hear, drank a
        still out of palms that shook.

18 months in ecstasy.

        Couple this tender close to
thrush, breath, rash, tears—

        What's the saying?
You can't compare apples to—
        I guess you had to be there.

A less flashy entrance, but same
        what-have-you and 62 falling sick.

        Source by speck, all open-wide—
            no detection for this flea.

Bit women hard on arms out-
        stretched over textiles, bit so deep
            they went outmind, all sticky-good.

And damn didn't they deserve it
—*ladies making dresses,* what next?

For your touch: taut eyes, and too
        much love for our sisters—our cistern.

It is more difficult to stop laughing
        during a moment that's candid—

        an intervention, a funeral, a sacrifice.
Is this thing on?

Reported dizzy, flu-like symptoms. Numb, they said,
        and spent days in catacomb embrace.

Love to each Freesia Warmblood, and regard
        that we do sting bc this one came
last ('67), and they called it an epidemic.

One man, so fearing, turned hooks,
        went fishing line, went shoe-string
all around his genuine member—*gone*
        wrong, he said, *gone missing, gone*

    N__ow that's a punchline

I am not trying to fashion
        photographs out of ghosts.

    Or take the wind out of
A perfectly wound spool.

We are as small as tree frogs,
        can oppose two fingers
             in a vise-like grip.

We taste eggs from leaves

and lay open-eyed, restless,

beneath hearsay and
      circumstance,

around heresy and
      stifled question:

             Does laughter die?
        Do gods grow old?

Outside, little girls shoot fat pigeons
      like small skyscrapers from below.

MANUAL FOR THE AFFLICTED
BY THE ERGOT FUNGI

Ergot fungi refers to a group of the genus Claviceps. The most prominent member of this group is Claviceps purpurea ("rye ergot fungus"), which can be commonly sourced from farmers' markets, the underside of the seats in defunct movie theaters, and the back room of most girl scout planning sessions particularly when in preparation of the annually much-anticipated cookie selling season. This fungus grows on rye and produces alkaloids that can cause ergotism in humans and other mammals who consume grains contaminated with its fruiting structure (called ergot sclerotium). One role of the sclerotia is to survive environmental extremes by rapidly increasing untraceable amounts of carbon monoxide in the human body. Symptoms of the ergot fungi are minute in comparison with its sister strains. Symptoms include long bouts of silence and an eventual degeneration of the human vocal cords. Most infected humans can exist for many years undetected among mass populations with the dormant properties of the ergot fungi. For the cause of identification and treatment, the dormant afflicted can be prompted to answer the following questions: 1) What was the name of the street you grew up on? and 2) What was the name of your first pet? to which the afflicted's answer will always be: Battle Hymn of the Republic.

Conversion Disorders in The Burn Pits, Please Take Flight

Conversion disorder is a mental condition in which a person has blindness, paralysis, or other nervous system (neurologic) symptoms that cannot be explained by medical evaluation. Conversion disorder symptoms may occur because of a psychological conflict.

social panics   fainting spells to twitching   shaking

     a trance state: call it   mass hysteria

(of course) it   starts   with   little girls   near puberty   or in

poor   working conditions   stifling

laughter   in the back of   a schoolroom   spinning

     tales   about   breaking   windows-   treaty   breaking

code-clocks   of   land   script   deed   an outing   of

the circumstance   an   out from   the lump   in the throat that

produces a sensation of   choking   if you   can think

     yourself   better   you   can also make   yourself   sick

with love   call it mania   for   a collective

     breakdown   a stress response against   a line of   history

that   speeds   fast   like red metal   towards dense fog

Build A Stage

And then lie across it—
slip-stream smile it over.

Ask few questions and take
a little more. Another dollar,

another day gathering signs:
a dream about big ants (the bug),

a noose hanging on a chair-back,
"Tiny Dancer" in the grocery aisle

rolling down freezer truths, beside
the white chickens—etcetera.

In my bedroom, a ladybug in
the summer means good luck.

Twenty ladybugs in the winter
means an infestation. Dark falls

on only half of the sky at a time.

Before you exit, friends, a preface:
certain mistakes cannot be

outdone by fire. I see your detail
and raise you circumstance,

serendipity, and water, water, air.

I Work on Roads

Many friends are sad
to see you go, but

don't fear being left
out of this refrain.

There are spaces—
enough for everyone.

Mine just happens
to be a cadenza,

sodden without
use for birdsong.

I nod, despite the
rain outside windows

that are made of
gold and plaster.

Please don't try the door
aside my delicate oration.

I find blooms in every
receptacle of refuse.

I find branches and
perfect shrubs where
my limbs used to be.

THE BURN PITS

It is possible to not know what lies
        underneath your skin.

The smell of gas, a minor accident—
        say fuel element failure.

We touch the pieces of dried grass
        on our descent, gather

back together a bundle in place
        of a vocabulary for names.

The great misstep, the human element:
        defect as communal birthright.

And how to remember what was
        never written? The memo

recommends departure, the memo
        suggests trace substances

still in the hold—hold them still
        leaking on roofs over tongue.

A stubborn breed, this animal. The
        only retribution: unforeseen fire.

We pour our mistakes into black pits,
        close the lid, and hope that the

smoke story might not reach the frontal
        lobes of chain-link and ashtray.

We drink the water, we brush

our teeth with the water,

and force another match into
        flame now growing dim by the

march of palms. No time to put it
        out and no time to waste on

exit music. There is a rumor I
        shouldn't tell you, but I will.

Count your hands by syllables,
        divide what's left by the root.

We are not who we say we are and
        the farther we go back, we're

tracing blood—filling bodies with
        this chemical breath, sending out

piecemeal parcels of well-lit verbs.

— Epilogue —

Savage Pageant: Jungleland Had Many Names

And now we are carving mythology out

of unremembered time. The recurrent
dream about Jungleland isn't about

tigers or Mabel or a roster of poorly
behaving men. We know memory,

like a trapped lion, must snack on
dry sandwiches to survive.

It would be nice to leave it alone,
the small lion to its tidy sandwich,

but here is the affliction

from stories better left unsaid:

the spectacle in the archive of harm,

the body left untouched for four hours,

of Flint and the shootings that no
longer receive another name.

We call a hundred mouths laughing
an epidemic.

We call a thousand killing bodies
a circumstance.

We are so far away

from it all, aren't we?

The plastic jungle
and the crass crate.

Yet here we sit like the
mannequins of young schoolgirls

imagining something out of thin air

our tongues curling around no-nation—

no sudden movements to call our own.

Historical genealogy timelines for Jungleland were partially extracted from, adapted from, or inspired by the Internet site, Weird California, its comment thread on Jungleland, as well as Jeffrey Wayne Maulhardt's *Jungleland*. Genealogies also include extracted quotes from Gaston Bachelard's *The Poetics of Space*.

Photograph, page 75: image taken by author of the current site of the Santa Susana Field Laboratory, area of the partial nuclear meltdown at Rocketdyne in 1959.

Google Maps: 2522 Pleasant Way is the address of the original Crowley House, which would later become Jungleland. The precise site of Jungleland today is unmarked and existed where the Thousand Oaks Civic Arts Plaza stands today.

Illustrations are based on archival photographs of Jungleland, Jayne Mansfield, the final performance of elephants in Ringling Bros. Circus (2016), Carhenge in Alliance, Nebraska, and a stock image of a Walmart greeter.

The first line of **THE DEAD LETTER OFFICE** uses part of a quotation from Woodrow Wilson from the first film screening of *The Birth of a Nation* at the White House in 1915. In response to the film screening, his full quotation reportedly was: "It's like writing history with lightning. My only regret is that it is all so terribly true."

AREA FOUR includes a description of psychogenic dystonia from a case study by Jean-Phillippe Langevin, Jesse M. Skoch, and Scott J. Sherman on "Deep brain stimulation of a patient with psychogenic movement disorder" (2016). Psychogenic dystonia is a condition, like "conversion disorder," that carries symptoms which are suspected to be caused by psychological factors rather than a brain disease.

TRACE LEAKAGE: JUNGLELAND: the text is extracted from the public comment thread on the homage website Weird California's entry about Jungleland. All entries have been anonymized and preserved in their original forms.

MISS PHOTOFLASH: the line *"Promises! Promises!"* refers to Jayne Mansfield's last film before her death.

COPS AND ROBBERS: epigraph is from an unofficial genealogy website for Daniel Boone's heritage (https://www.family-genealogy-online.com/little/boone.html). George Boone is the first recorded member of the Boone family lineage.

ARIEL is after Sylvia Plath and Safiya Sinclair.

N 34° 10.362 W 118° 50.772 are the GPS coordinates of the Crowley House.

ROADSIDE ATTRACTIONS refers to the 1773 killing of James Boone (Daniel Boone's son) and Henry Russell in "History of Scott County, Virginia" by Robert M. Addington. The historical roadside marker commemorating the event has changed its location three times because of conflicting claims on where events occurred. More than once, it has been anonymously dug up in the middle of the night and replanted.

NEWBURY PARK HIGH SCHOOL refers to the school's current mascot, the "Panthers," which was supposedly inspired by the nearby panther that had escaped from Jungleland. This poem also references victims of Kenneth Bianchi and Angelo Bruono, collectively known as the "Hillside Stranger" in the 1970s. The murders began with the deaths of three sex workers who were found strangled and dumped naked on hillsides northeast of Los Angeles.

CONVERSION DISORDER: the epigraph definition of "conversion disorder" is from an article, "Conversion Disorder: Definition, Symptoms, and Treatment" by Kathleen Smith. The term was coined by Sigmund Freud in his *Studies on Hysteria*.

ERGOT FUNGI: parts of the poem are borrowed from the Wikipedia page on "ergot fungi," a type of contaminating fungus that is rumored to be an understudied, potential cause for psychogenic illness—specifically episodes associated with the Salem Witch Trials.

SAVAGE PAGEANT: JUNGLELAND HAD MANY NAMES includes references to the murder of Michael Brown by a white police officer in 2014 and the ongoing water crisis in Flint, Michigan.

Lastly, I am indebted to Aracelis Girmay's *the black maria* and Diana Khoi Nguyen's *Ghost Of* for re-teaching me the mobility of death and trauma.

ACKNOWLEDGEMENTS

Grateful acknowledgement to the editors of the following publications in which these poems, sometimes in earlier iterations, have appeared:

Heavy Feather Review: "Strange Beasts"
Lute & Drum: "Newbury Park High School," "World Jungle Compound"
Pleiades: "Savage Pageant: A Genealogy"
Tethered by Letters: "Mass Psychogenic Illness (case study)"
Tupelo Quarterly: "The Burn Pits," "Daniel Boone's Bones," "Name Numer-ology K-Hole: 11 Weeks"

I am so thankful for the work and attention of Chris Tonelli, benevolent bear-poet holding infinite space for poetry in the unassuming confines of Raleigh, North Carolina. Your encouragement has fueled my most valuable bouts of literary mania.

Thank you also to all the folks at Birds, LLC for taking on a messy text in good faith and for cultivating a rare space of intimacy and friendship in the calculation of contemporary publishing. Gratitude to Zoe Norvell for the book's cover design and interior design. Thank you to all of my friends, friend-editors, and teachers that have helped me push this book into shape and out into the world while I was trying to bring a small person and a critical, doctoral dissertation into it at the same time. Thank you to Joseph Donahue and Nathaniel Mackey for always humoring my some-times-formidable affect. Thank you to Priscilla Wald, for showing me it isn't wrong to want it all. Thank you to John Paul Stadler, Lauren Hunter, Laura Jaramillo, Brian Howe, Michelle Dove, Hannah VanderHart, Zach Levine, Joanna Penn Cooper, David Dulceany, Lightsey Darst, Ken Taylor, I. Augustus Durham, Adra Raine, Amanda Dahill-Moore, Dylan White, Trisha Federis, Sylvia Herbold, and all of the North Carolina poets and creatives that have heard several of these poems read aloud ad nauseum and with continued interest. Thank you to Fred Moten for your kind words after watching me shake through my first public reading. Thank you to all of the poets that visited Durham, North Carolina for the Little Corner Reading Series; your readings shaped me in innumerable ways. Gratitude

for Vi Khi Nao, poetry-sister, for bánh xèo and community. Thank you to
Dorothea Lasky, for your voice and the flash in the pan that kept me going.
Thank you to Bhanu Kapil for your enabling excess and your shocking
tenderness.

Thank you to the ghosts of California and for my mother who showed me
how to know them. For my sisters, and their endless reserve of laughter
and forgiveness. For my father, for history and always reading the books
I've sent. Thank you to Evan and Annie for their persistent confidence and
interest. Thank you, thank you.

Thank you, Kiki, for repositioning your naps. The most thanks to Daniel,
for always being Daniel—lovelight and the unassuming muse as graceful
Whooping Crane. And for Adrian, of course, for writing this with me
while you grew and grew.

PHOTO: ZOE LITAKER

JESSICA Q. STARK is a mixed-race, Vietnamese poet and scholar originally from California. She received her PhD in English at Duke University, a Master's of English from Saint Louis University, and a B.A. in English from the University of California, Berkeley. She is the author of three poetry chapbooks, the latest titled *Vasilisa the Wise* (Ethel Zine Press, 2018). Her chapbook manuscript, *The Liminal Parade*, was selected by Dorothea Lasky for Heavy Feather's Double Take Poetry Prize in 2016. Her poems have appeared in *Hobart, Tupelo Quarterly*, *Potluck*, *Glass Poetry Journal*, and others. She writes an ongoing poetry zine called *INNANET* and works as an Assistant Poetry Editor for *AGNI*. Find her on Twitter @jezzbah.